Tadpole to Frog

Animals Grow Up

Shira Evans

NATIONAL GEOGRAPHIC

Washington, D.C.

How to Use This Book

Reading together is fun! When older and younger readers share the experience, it opens the door to new learning. As you read together, talk about what you learn.

YOU READ

This side is for a parent, older sibling, or older friend. Before reading each page, take a look at the words and pictures. Talk about what you see. Point out words that might be hard for the younger reader.

I READ

This side is for the younger reader.

As you read, look for the bolded words. Talk about them before you read. In each chapter, the bolded words are: Chapter 1: nouns • Chapter 2: describing words • Chapter 3: action words • Chapter 4: nouns • Chapter 5: action words

At the end of each chapter, do the activity together.

YOUR TURN!

Think about how an egg turns into a butterfly. Then act out the different steps! Say what you are doing.

Table of Contents

Babies Grow Up

YOU READ

All living things have a life cycle.
Animal **babies** start small.
Then they grow bigger and bigger.

Babies change as they grow.

Some babies look like **adults**.
Others look very different.
The difference might only be size.
Or it might be shape and color, too.

Soon, all babies will grow into **adults**. Then they have babies, too. The cycle starts again.

This butterfly is laying eggs.

YOUR TURN!

Look at the animals.
Which ones are babies?
Which are adults?
Talk about how you know.

CHAPTER 2

Just Like Me!

YOU READ

Many baby animals look like their parents, only smaller. A mother giraffe is much **taller** than her baby. They both have long necks to reach leaves, though. They both have spots, too.

 The baby will grow **taller.**
Then it will look just like
its mom.

YOU
READ

When an alligator hatches, its skin is hard and bumpy like its mother's. These scales keep it safe from the hot sun. The baby has **sharp** teeth like an adult, too.

The baby hunts with its **sharp** teeth. It eats and eats. Soon it will grow as big as its mother.

YOU READ

Baby owls are born with soft, fluffy feathers called "down." The down keeps them warm. As the babies grow bigger, they will get **strong** feathers. Soon they will look exactly like their mother.

READ

The mother brings the babies food. Soon they will be **strong**. They will fly away.

YOUR TURN!

Match the baby animals to the adults. Use your finger to make a line from each baby to the right adult.

BABIES

ADULTS

CHAPTER 3

Fabulous Frogs!

YOU READ A baby frog doesn't look like an adult frog at all! It starts off as a tiny egg in the water. When it's ready, the egg will **hatch**.

Frogs lay many eggs at one time.

 Frog eggs **hatch** into little tadpoles.

Tadpoles are born with gills, which they use to breathe in the water. They **swim** by moving their tail back and forth.

They eat and grow as they **swim**. They do not have legs yet.

YOU READ Soon the tadpole will leave the water to live on land. Before it can, it will need to get bigger. Its lungs need to **grow**. The tadpole will use its lungs to breathe air.

 Its front and back legs start to **grow**, too. It will need legs to hop on land.

The frog's gills disappear. Its tail disappears, too! Now it has lungs to breathe and legs to **jump**. Finally, the frog can live out of the water.

READ

It uses its strong legs to **jump** from place to place. The tadpole has turned into a frog!

YOUR TURN!

Look at the frog life cycle. Point to each picture. Use the words in the word bank to talk about each stage.

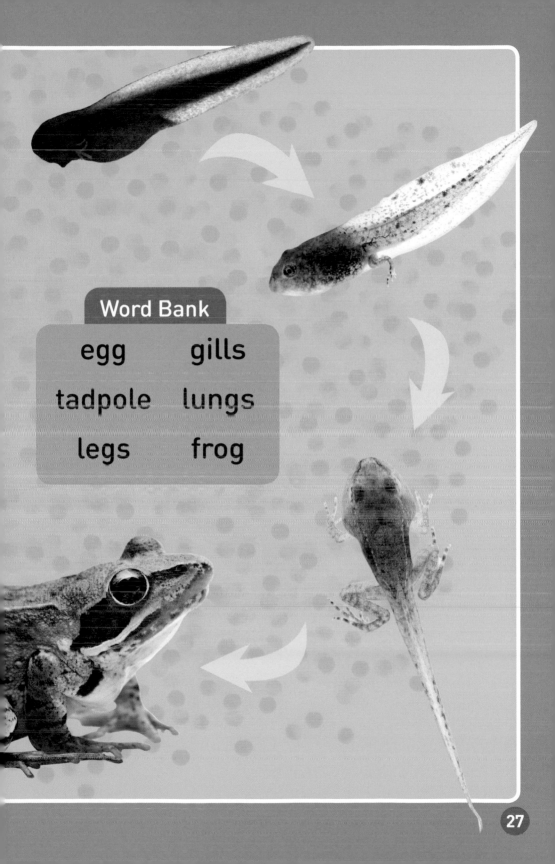

CHAPTER 4

Beautiful Butterflies

YOU READ

Like a frog, a butterfly starts life as an **egg**. First an adult butterfly lays an egg on a leaf. It will stay safe there.

1

 Soon the **egg** hatches. A tiny caterpillar comes out.

YOU READ

The **caterpillar** has many legs. It crawls up and down plant stems all day, munching on leaves as it goes along.

The **caterpillar** is hungry. It eats and eats. It gets bigger and bigger.

When the caterpillar is big enough, it becomes a **pupa**. A tough shell forms around it to keep it safe. Now the pupa stays in one place.

Butterfly pupas attach themselves to plants or other safe places as they change.

The pupa changes color as it grows.

 Inside its shell, the **pupa** changes.

YOU READ

Soon, the animal inside the shell begins to break out. It is no longer a caterpillar, though! It has turned into a **butterfly**.

 The **butterfly** doesn't munch on leaves now. It flies from flower to flower and drinks.

YOUR TURN!

egg

①

Think about how an egg turns into a butterfly. Then act out the different steps! Say what you are doing.

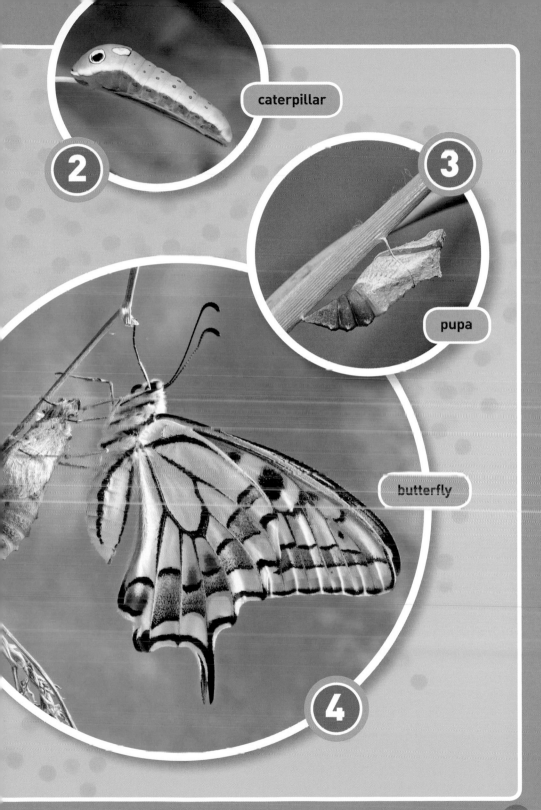

2

caterpillar

3

pupa

butterfly

4

CHAPTER 5

Grow Up and Fly Away!

YOU
READ

A baby dragonfly doesn't look at all like its parents, either. An adult dragonfly lives on land. But a baby hatches from an egg and **swims** underwater. It breathes with gills, like a tadpole.

A baby dragonfly lives in the water.

Some baby dragonflies change their skin more than 15 times!

A baby dragonfly **swims** and eats. It changes its skin as it gets bigger.

An adult dragonfly dries its wings next to its old skin.

YOU READ

Then the baby dragonfly crawls out of the water and up a stem. It changes its skin one last time. Finally, it's an adult, with wings to **fly**.

The adult lets its new wings dry. Then it **flies** away!

YOU
READ Have you ever wondered what a baby ladybug looks like? You might be surprised! It looks long and spiny. It **crawls** along and eats. Soon, though, it will turn into an adult ladybug.

 Adult ladybugs can **crawl,** too. But then they open their wings and fly away!

43

YOU READ

Not all babies look like their parents. Some babies have different shapes and colors. Sometimes they do different things. But all babies grow and **change**.

 Babies eat and get bigger. In time, they will **change** into adults. They won't look like babies anymore!

YOUR TURN!

Choose an animal. Tell how it changes from baby to adult. Use the words in the word bank.

Word Bank

first

then

finally

To Sam and Alex, whose love of nature continues to inspire me —S.E.

Designed by YAY! Design

The author and publisher gratefully acknowledge the expert literacy review of this book by Kimberly Gillow, principal, Milan Area Schools, Michigan, and the fact-checking and research of this book by Michelle Harris.

Trade paperback ISBN: 978-1-4263-3203-6
Reinforced library binding ISBN: 978-1-4263-3204-3

Illustration Credits

Cover, Jonathan Fife/Getty Images; 1, paylessimages/Getty Images; 3, proxyminder/Getty Images; 4, Luke Wait/Shutterstock; 5 (UP), Eric Isselée/Shutterstock; 5 (LO), Gerard Lacz/REX/Shutterstock; 6, Andrey Nekrasov/imageBROKER/REX/Shutterstock; 7, Muhammad Naaim/Shutterstock; 8 (LE), StuPorts/Getty Images; 8 (RT), Mitsuaki Iwago/Minden Pictures; 9 (UP), Anup Shah/Minden Pictures; 9 (CTR LE), Jon Graham/Shutterstock; 9 (CTR RT), gnomeandi/Shutterstock; 9 (LO), bookguy/Getty Images; 10–11, Sean Crane/Minden Pictures; 12 (UP), Will E. Davis/Shutterstock; 12 (LO), David Kjaer/Nature Picture Library; 13, Orhan Cam/Shutterstock; 14–15, Peter Lilja/Getty Images; 15, Marc Gottenbos/Minden Pictures; 16 (UP LE), Andy Dean Photography/Shutterstock; 16 (UP RT), LifetimeStock/Shutterstock; 16 (CTR), DenisNata/Shutterstock; 16 (LO LE), Anan Kaewkhammul/Shutterstock; 16 (LO RT), Gelpi/Shutterstock; 17 (UP), KAMONRAT/Shutterstock; 17 (CTR LE), Andy Dean Photography/Shutterstock; 17 (CTR), Gelpi/Shutterstock; 17 (CTR RT), Melinda Fawver/Shutterstock; 17 (LO), Eric Isselée/Shutterstock; 18–19, David Tipling/Nature Picture Library; 19, Fabio Liverani/Nature Picture Library; 20–21, Harry Rogers/Getty Images; 22, Thomas Marent/Minden Pictures; 23, FLPA/REX/Shutterstock; 24, Stephen Dalton/Minden Pictures; 25, Dale Sutton/2020VISION/Nature Picture Library; 26–27, GlobalP/Getty Images; 28–29, Kim Taylor/Nature Picture Library; 30–31, Silvia Reiche/Minden Pictures; 32, blickwinkel/Alamy Stock Photo; 33 (UP), blickwinkel/Alamy Stock Photo; 33 (LO), Education Images/UIG via Getty Images; 34, Silvia Reiche/Minden Pictures; 35 (UP), Kim Taylor/Nature Picture Library; 35 (LO), Matauw/Getty Images; 36, Somyot Mali-ngam/Shutterstock; 37 (UP), Terryfic3D/Getty Images; 37 (CTR), image2roman/Getty Images; 37 (LO), mauribo/Getty Images; 38, VitalisG/Getty Images; 39, Steve Downer/ARDEA; 40, Alex Huizinga/Minden Pictures; 41, Rene Krekels/Minden Pictures; 42, Anteromite/Shutterstock; 43, irin-k/Shutterstock; 44, Volodymyr Goinyk/Shutterstock; 45 (UP), Julie Lubick/Shutterstock; 45 (LO), vkilikov/Shutterstock; 46, Butterfly Hunter/Shutterstock; 47 (UP), Subbotina Anna/Shutterstock; 47 (CTR), Alex Staroseltsev/Shutterstock; 47 (LO), halimqd/Shutterstock; Top border and background (throughout), Jane Burton/Minden Pictures

National Geographic supports K–12 educators with ELA Common Core Resources. Visit natgeoed.org/commoncore for more information.

Printed in the United States of America
18/WOR/1